Of the legendary four great Russian poets of her generation (others were Akhmatova, Mandelstam, and Pasternak) at the beginning of the twentieth century, Marina Tsvetaeva has always seemed to me the most mysterious. Of course they were all mysterious—what great poet, indeed what individual person is not?—but I have turned from reading translations (I read no Russian) of her poems and writings, and from writings about her and her tormented story—and from reading them gratefully—with a feeling that, vivid and searing though they may have been, she had been in them like a ghost in a cloud, and was gone again.

This new selection from her poems and prose, a "homage" to her by Ilya Kaminsky and Jean Valentine, brought me a closer and more intimate sense of her and of her voice and presence than I had before. Besides, if we had not had Ilya Kaminsky's own radiant first book, *Dancing in Odessa,* and the singular unfolding over several decades of Jean Valentine's haunting poetry, this brief representation of Tsvetaeva's life, fate, and the poetry that is inseparable from them, would have made their talents and their stature unmistakable. This *Dark Elderberry Branch* is magic.

W.S. MERWIN

DARK

ELDERBERRY

BRANCH

DARK

POEMS *of*

ELDERBERRY

MARINA TSVETAEVA

BRANCH

A Reading by **ILYA KAMINSKY** *and* **JEAN VALENTINE**

Alice James Books
FARMINGTON, MAINE
www.alicejamesbooks.org

10 9 8 7 6 5 4 3 2

Alice James Books are published by Alice James Poetry Cooperative, Inc., an affiliate
of the University of Maine at Farmington.

Alice James Books
238 Main Street
Farmington, ME 04938
www.alicejamesbooks.org

Library of Congress Cataloging-in-Publication Data

Tsvetaeva, Marina, 1892-1941, author.
  [Works. English. Selections. 2012]
  Dark elderberry branch / poems of Marina Tsvetaeva ; a reading by Ilya
Kaminsky and Jean Valentine.
      pages ; cm
  Includes bibliographical references and index.
  ISBN 978-1-882295-94-4 (paperback : alkaline paper)
  I. Kaminsky, Ilya, 1977-, translator, writer of added commentary. II. Valentine,
Jean, translator. III. Title.
  PG3476.T75A2 2012
  891.71'42--dc23
                              2012021490

Alice James Books gratefully acknowledges support from individual donors, private
foundations, the University of Maine at Farmington, and the National Endowment for
the Arts.

Contributions for this reprint were made by The Frank M. Barnard Foundation.

ART WORKS.
arts.gov

Cover Art: *Marina Tsvetaeva with her dog in Savoy,* Fine Art Images.

TABLE OF CONTENTS

Rhythms of the Soul: Marina Tsvetaeva
An Introduction by Stephanie Sandler   xi

There are four of us
by Anna Akhmatova   xvii

Afterword

ACKNOWLEDGMENTS

Some of these poems, sometimes in different versions, have appeared, or are forthcoming, in:

Poetry
The Penguin Anthology of 20ᵗʰ Century Russian Poetry (Penguin)
20ᵗʰ Century Russian Modernist Poets: A Reader (Tupelo Press)
Ecco Anthology of International Poetry (Harper Collins)

RHYTHMS OF THE SOUL:

MARINA TSVETAEVA

There are many souls in me, Marina Tsvetaeva once wrote, and readers of her work often have the feeling that spiritual forces compete in every line she ever wrote. The emotional intensity of her writing, whether in prose or in poetry, seems startlingly able to bend her language into unimaginable new shapes. That linguistic fearlessness makes her a challenge for translators, but readers of this volume will palpably sense the sheer force of her language. In choosing and ordering these writings, Ilya Kaminsky and Jean Valentine create force fields across the poems and prose fragments; they have lifted a small number of texts from the massive Tsvetaeva legacy, creating luminous new versions for us to behold. The translations attain a kind of light-showered clarity before our eyes, with each scrap of text commanding our focused attention as if nothing else mattered.

Tsvetaeva left a stunning amount of work for such a short and trouble-filled life. Born in 1892 into a musical and intellectual family, reared in an atmosphere where art must always have seemed her destiny, she was as fierce in her emotional attachments as she was in her quests for artistic expression. She married young, to Sergei Efron, and although her life would include affairs of searing passion and high drama, she loved Efron to the end. She followed him to Europe in emigration in 1922 and then back to the Soviet Union in 1939. Her return was a dreadful choice, but there were not a lot of good alternatives in Europe in those years. Efron was arrested in Moscow and executed; their daughter, Ariadna, who had been jailed earlier in the 1930s, was rearrested and sent to the camps. Their son Mur was soon killed in the Second World War. Tsvetaeva herself would die in 1941, in evacuation and by her own hand. Her sister, Anastasia, who survived until the 1990s, was not spared her share of suffering (including two terms in the labor camps). But because of Anastasia Tsvetaeva's efforts and those of Ariadna Efron, we have Tsvetaeva's manuscripts, including a treasure trove of notebooks and drafts. Some of the most startling pages in this volume come from those notebooks, or, as they are called here, daybooks. These sentences read as if direct transcriptions of the insights and recognitions that make writing possible. They allow readers in English to glimpse something of Tsvetaeva's creative laboratory.

You must write as if God is watching you, wrote Tsvetaeva in one of the fragments. And although her work has the electric charge of this ever-present sublime audience, many of her poems and most of her essays are in fact addressed to individuals to whom she was deeply connected. She felt profound poetic kinships with Pasternak and Rilke, and there were many poets among her addressees. There was the great Osip Mandelstam: their 1916 romance produced legendary poems by both of them. Her poems to him show Tsvetaeva both charming and charmed:

Where does this tenderness come from?
And what will I do with it? Young
stranger, poet, in this city of strangers:
you and your eyelashes — longer than anyone's.

Those eyelashes appear in another poem, in which Tsvetaeva says to Mandelstam that he has the god of poetry within him. In that same year, 1916 (it was a year of phenomenal poetic output for her), Tsvetaeva wrote a cycle of poems to Alexander Blok, adored by so many poets of her era. She was fascinated by the poetic persona adopted by Blok, but her poems captured the linguistic magic of his poetry, which for her inheres even in his name. To say that name is to feel an icicle on the tongue, she wrote, evoking the bracing pleasure of saying his poems to oneself. In 1916 she wrote poems to Anna Akhmatova as well, Akhmatova who would later associate the "dark elderberry branch" with Tsvetaeva's own name.

Not all of Tsvetaeva's acts of dedicated speech were to such worthy addressees—the long *Poem of the End* and its twin, *Poem of the Mountain*, were prompted by the breakup of a rather tawdry affair with Konstantin Rodzevich when Tsvetaeva was living in Prague in the 1920s, but the resulting verse was no less staggering than the 1916 cycles. By the 1930s, the poet was writing more prose than poetry (and readers may find much more of that prose, in the volumes *A Captive Spirit*, tr. J. Marin King, and *Art in the Light of Conscience*, tr. Angela Livingstone); as this book shows so well, the two forms of expression were remarkably close in spirit. Tsvetaeva finds ways to make prose words vibrate with the high frequencies more readily found in lyric poetry.

When we read Tsvetaeva, the worlds of Moscow before the Revolution and during the Civil War, and of émigré Prague and Paris, are recreated. She makes these places, and the people she knew, come alive. But her work also lets readers sense the distinctive creative energy of her own psyche. We follow her emotions of love and jealousy, of loss and rebellion, and we experience as if alongside her the travails of writing and thinking, the refusals to swim on the current of human spines, as one of her poems to Czechoslovakia has it. One should not underestimate the clarity of mind that grounded Tsvetaeva's emotions, nor the firmness of spirit that sustained her through harsh times. In offering us their versions of Tsvetaeva's writings, Jean Valentine and Ilya Kaminsky describe their work as homage—and it is a fitting tribute to this most rare poet.

—STEPHANIE SANDLER

In homage to Marina Tsvetaeva

There are four of us

On paths of air I seem to overhear
two friends, two voices, talking in their turn,

Did I say two?... There by the eastern wall,
where criss-cross shoots of brambles trail,
—O look!—that fresh dark elderberry branch
is like a letter from Marina in the mail.

—ANNA AKHMATOVA
NOVEMBER 1961 (IN DELIRIUM)

from *Poems of Akhmatova*, tr. Stanley Kunitz and Max Hayward.
Boston: Little Brown and Company, 1973.

DARK

ELDERBERRY

BRANCH

from Poems for Moscow

From my hands—take this city not made by hands,
my strange, my beautiful brother.

Take it, church by church—all forty times forty churches,
and flying up the roofs, the small pigeons;

and Spassky Gates—and gates, and gates—
where the Orthodox take off their hats;

and the Chapel of Stars—refuge chapel—
where the floor is—polished by tears;

take the circle of the five cathedrals,
my coal, my soul; the domes wash us in their darkgold,

and on your shoulders, from the red clouds,
the Mother of God will drop her own thin coat,

and you will rise, happened of wonderpowers
—never ashamed you loved me.

MARCH 31 1916

1

"I won't leave you!" Only God can say this—or a peasant with milk in Moscow, winter 1918.

EARTHLY TRACES, 1919-20

My "I don't want to" is always "I cannot." In me there is no arbitrariness. "I cannot"—and meek eyes.

EARTHLY TRACES, 1919-20

I bless our hands' daily labor

I bless our hands' daily labor, bless
sleep every night.
Bless night every night.

And the coat, your coat, my coat,
half dust, half holes.
And I bless the peace

in a stranger's house—the bread in a stranger's oven.

1918

I am happy living simply

I am happy living simply
like a clock, or a calendar.
Or a woman, thin,
lost—as any creature. To know

the spirit is my beloved. To arrive on earth—swift
as a ray of light, or a look.
To live as I write: spare—the way
God asks me—and friends do not.

1919

In the Commissariat

I, innocently: "Is it difficult to be an instructor?"
My co-worker in the Commissariat, a woman, a communist: "Not at all difficult! You just stand up on a trash can—and yell, yell, yell."

EARTHLY TRACES, 1919-20

My little thefts in the Commissariat: two gorgeous checkered notebooks (yellow, bright), a whole box of quills to write with, a glass bubble of red English ink. I am writing with it now.

EARTHLY TRACES, 1919-20

from Poems for Moscow

Seven hills—like seven bells,
seven bells toll in the seven bell towers.
All forty times forty churches, all seven hills
of bells, every one of them counted, like pillows.

I was born in the ringing of bells
on the saint's day of John the Theologian.
Over the wattle fence, our gingerbread house—
dropped its crumbs for Saint John the Theologian.

I loved it first: the first ringing—
the nuns sweeping to mass in the warmth of sleep—
the crack of the fire catching in the stove—
seven bells, seven bell towers.

Come with me, people of Moscow,
you crazy, looting, flagellant mob!
And priest—place on my tongue
all of Moscow, the city of bells!

1916

I don't eavesdrop, I listen in. Like a doctor to someone's chest. And, often, you tap, and there is no echo!

EARTHLY TRACES, 1919-20

It was forbidden for the bourgeoisie to use horses for removing snow from the streets. So the bourgeoisie, without a second thought, hired themselves a camel. And the camel hauled the snow. And the soldiers laughed out loud. (I saw this with my own eyes, on Arbat Street.)

EARTHLY TRACES, 1919-20

Where does such tenderness come from?

Where does such tenderness come from?
These aren't the first curls
I've wound around my finger—
I've kissed lips darker than yours.

The sky is washed, dark
(where does such tenderness come from?).
Other eyes have eyed—
and stolen from my eyes.

But I've never heard words like this
in the night
(where does such tenderness come from?)
with my head on your chest, rest.

Where does this tenderness come from?
And what will I do with it? Young
stranger, poet, in this city of strangers:
you and your eyelashes—longer than anyone's.

1916

A kiss on the forehead

A kiss on the forehead—erases misery.
I kiss your forehead.

A kiss on the eyes—lifts sleeplessness.
I kiss your eyes.

A kiss on the lips—is a drink of water.
I kiss your lips.

A kiss on the forehead—erases memory.

1917

from Poems for Blok

Your name is a—bird in my hand,
a piece of ice on my tongue.
The lips' quick opening.
Your name—four letters.
A ball caught in flight,
a silver bell in my mouth.

A stone thrown into a silent lake
is—the sound of your name.
The light click of hooves at night
—your name.
Your name at my temple
—sharp click of a cocked gun.

Your name—impossible—
kiss on my eyes,
the chill of closed eyelids.
Your name—a kiss of snow.
Blue gulp of icy spring water.
With your name—sleep deepens.

APRIL 15 1916

The cruel words of Blok about very early Akhmatova: "Akhmatova writes poems as if a man is watching her, but you have to write as if God is watching you."

"PRAYER," *ART IN THE LIGHT OF CONSCIENCE*, 1932

from Poems for Akhmatova

I won't fall behind you. I'm the guard.
You—the prisoner. Our fate is the same.
And here in the same open emptiness
they command us the same—Go away.

So—I lean against nothing.
I see it.
Let me go, my prisoner,
to walk over towards that pine tree.

JUNE 1916

The mysterious disappearance of the photographer on Tverskaya Street, who long and stubbornly took (free) pictures of the Soviet elite.

EARTHLY TRACES, 1919-20

Not long ago, in Kuntsevo, I suddenly crossed myself when I saw an oak. Evidently, the source of prayer is not fear, but delight.

EARTHLY TRACES, 1919-20

You throw back your head

You throw back your head
because you are proud, and a liar.
What a smiling boy this February has thrown at me!

You throw back your head.
Bumped into by boys looking for money,
we walk, two pompous kids, around my native city.

You throw back your head.
Whose finger, whose
fingers have touched your eyelashes?

Sweet boy, and when, and how many times,
your lips have kissed—
I do not ask. My thirst

must honor the poetry and God inside you, ten years old!
(You throw back your head.)
Let's wait by the river—it rinses

the bright beads of the streetlights:
you throw back your head,
my fool, running free—disappear. Forgive.

1916

I wake with the sun. Quickly jump into my huge red dress (the color of cardinals—fire!). Write a note to N. Carefully open the door, and—horror!—an enormous double bed, and on it many sleeping bodies. I step back. Then, deciding suddenly, with big quiet steps I head for the opposite door. Turn the handle.

"And who have we here?"

On the bed sits a man—disheveled head, unbuttoned shirt, he watches me.

"This is I. By accident I slept in this house, and now I am going away."

"But comrade!"

"For God's sake, forgive me. I did not think, that—I think, that—I, evidently, have gotten into the wrong place."

And not waiting for a reply, I disappear.

Later heard from N: the man took me for a red ghost. The specter of the Revolution, disappearing with the first rays of the sun! He couldn't stop laughing as he told me about it.

DAYBOOK, MOSCOW, 1918-19

I know the truth

I know the truth! Give up all the other truths.
No time on earth for people to kill each other.
Look—it's evening; look, it's nearly night. No more
of your talk, poets, lovers, generals.

Now no wind, and the earth is sprinkled with drizzle,
and soon the blizzard of stars will go quiet.
And soon, soon, to sleep, under the earth, all of us,
us who alive on earth don't let us sleep.

1915

Assassination Attempt on Lenin

Evening of the same day. My roommate, communist Zaks, bursting into the kitchen:

"And are you happy?"

I look down—not from shyness, of course: afraid to offend him. (Lenin has been shot. The White Army has entered the city, all the communists have been hanged, Zaks first among them.) Already I feel the generosity of the winning side.

"And you—are you very upset?"

"I?" (Tremble of shoulders.) "For us, Marxists, who don't recognize personal identity in history, this, in general terms, is not important—Lenin or someone else. It is you, the representatives of bourgeois culture," (new spasm), "with your Napoleons and your Caesars," (a devilish smile), ". . . but for us, us, us, you understand . . . Today it is Lenin, and tomorrow it is—"

Offended on Lenin's behalf (!), I say nothing. Awkward pause. And then, quickly-quickly, he says:

"—Marina, I've got some sugar here, three-quarters of a pound, I don't need it; perhaps you would take it for your daughter?"

DAYBOOK, MOSCOW, 1918-19

from **Poem of the End**

Outside of town! Understand? Out!
We're outside the walls. Outside life—
where life shambles to lepers.
The Jew-ish quarter.

It's a hundred times an honor
to stand with the Jews—
for anyone not scum.

Outside the walls, we stand. Outside life—
the Jew-ish quarter.

Life is for converts only!
Judases of all faiths.
Go find a leper colony!
Or hell! Anywhere—just not

life—life loves only liars,
lifts its sheep to blades.
I stomp on my birth certificate,
rub out my name!

Go find a leper colony! With David's star, I stand—
I spit on my passport.

And back in the town they're saying, It's only right—
the Jews don't *want* to live!

Ghetto of the chosen! The wall and ditch.
No mercy. In this most Christian of worlds
all poets—are Jews.

PRAGUE, 1924

For complete concurrence of souls there needs to be a concurrence of breath, for what is breath, if not the rhythm of the soul? So, for humans to understand one another, they must walk or lie side by side.

ON LOVE, 1917

from New Year's Letter

Happy New Year—light—country—home!
The first letter to you in your new
—to call it lush is wrong—
your loud place, your resonant
place—the first letter to you from yesterday.

*

Skip the details. Move on. Expediency.
New Year at the door. Who do I clink glasses with
across the table? What
am I in the New Year
with this dying rhyme: "Rainer—there."

Happy new earth, Rainer, town, Rainer!
Happy furthermost cape of all seen—
happy new eye, Rainer, ear, ear, Rainer!

*

Is heaven like a snowed-in amphitheater?
Is it true what I knew, that God is a *growing* baobab? And God's not

lost? Another God over him? And above him, further
up, another?

—How is writing, Rainer? Where there's no desk for your elbow, for your palm
no forehead—send a telegram! —Rainer—are you happy with sea changes
with your rhymes? With strangers in your line? What is death,
Rainer? Bone-learned language: assonances, sentences.
Will we meet? —Our words will meet,
in the ocean water, Rainer, when the earth calls the bells
on my day and there is no desk
for the elbow, for my palm, no forehead.
Go to the ladder—bring poems—
so I won't drop them, I hold up my cupped palm,
above the Rhine and Rarogne, above your grave,
above the stone separation,
deliver this to Rainer—Maria—Rilke's hand.

BELLEVUE, FEBRUARY 7 1927

But today I want Rilke to speak—through me. In the vernacular, this is known as translation. (Germans put it so much better—*nachdichten*—to pave over the road, over instantaneously vanishing traces.) But translation has another meaning. To translate not just into (i.e., into the Russian language), but across (a river). I translate Rilke into Russian, as he will someday translate me to the other world.

By hand—across the river.

1929

from An Attempt at Jealousy

How is your life with that other one?
Simpler, is it? A stroke of the oars
and a long coastline—
and the memory of me

is soon a drifting island
(not in—the ocean—in the air!).
Souls—you will be sisters—
sisters, not lovers.

How is your life with an *ordinary*
woman? Without the god inside her?
The queen supplanted—

How do you breathe now?
Flinch, waking up?
What do you do, poor man?

"Hysterics and interruptions—
enough! I'll rent my own house!"
How *is* your life with that other,
you, my own.

Is the breakfast egg boiled?
(If you get sick, don't blame me!)

How is it, living with a postcard?
You who stood on Sinai.

How's your life with a tourist
on Earth? Her rib (*do* you love her?)
—to your liking?

Is it life? Do you cough?
Do you hum to drown out the mice in your mind?

How do you live with cheap goods: is the market rising?
How's kissing plaster-dust?

Are you bored with her new body?
How's it going, with an earthly woman,
with no sixth sense?

                    Are you happy?
No? In a shallow pit—how is your life,
my beloved. Hard as mine
with another man?

1924

To love—is to see a man as God intended him, and his parents failed to make him.

To fall out of love—is to see, instead of him: a table, a chair.

EARTHLY TRACES, 1919-20.

from The Desk (1)

Thirty years together—
clearer than love.
I know your grain by heart,
you know my lines.

Wasn't it you who wrote them on my face?
You ate paper, you taught me:
There's no tomorrow. You taught me:
Today, today.

Money, bills, love letters, money, bills,
you stood in a blizzard of oak.
Kept saying: For every word you want
today, today.

God, you kept saying,
doesn't accept bits and bills.
Nnh, when they lay my body out, my fool, my
desk, let it be on you.

1933

from The Desk (2)

Fair enough: you people have eaten me,
I—wrote you down.
They'll lay you out on a dinner table,
me—on this desk.

I've loved living with little.
There are dishes I've never tried.
But you, you people eat slowly, and often;
you eat and eat.

Everything was decided for us
back in the ocean:
our places of action,
our places of gratitude.

You—with belches, I—with books,
with truffles, you. With pencil, I,
you and your olives, me and my rhyme,
with pickles, you. I, with poems.

At your head—funeral candles
like thick-legged asparagus:
your road out of this world
a dessert table's striped cloth.

They will smoke Havana cigars
on your left side and your right;
your body will be dressed
in the best Dutch linen.

And—not to waste such expensive cloth,
they will shake you out,
along with the crumbs and bits of food,
into the grave, hole.

You—stuffed capon, I—pigeon.
Gunpowder, your soul, at the autopsy.
And I will be laid out bare
—two wings to cover me.

1933

You can't buy me. That is the whole point. To buy is to buy oneself off. You can't buy yourself off from me. You can buy me only with the whole sky in yourself. The whole sky in which, perhaps, there is no place for me.

ABOUT GRATITUDE, 1919

from Poems to Czechoslovakia

Black mountain, black mountain
Ispania v krovi
black mountain blacks
Spain's blood—

Black mountain blocks
Czhechia's eyes.
Time—time—time
to give back to God his ticket.

I refuse to—be. In
the madhouse of the inhumans
I refuse to—live. To swim

on the current of human spines.
I don't need holes in my ears,
no need for seeing eyes.
I refuse to swim on the current of human spines.

To your mad world—one answer: I refuse.

*

They took—suddenly—and took—openly—
took mountains—and took their entrails,
they took coal, and steel they took,
they took lead, and crystal.

And sugar they took, and took the clover,
they took the West, and they took the North,
they took the beehive, and took the haystack.
Vari—they took, and the Tatras—they took,

they took the South from us, and the East.
They took our fingers—and fingered our friends—
but we stand up—
as long as there's spit in our mouths!

MAY 9 1939

Today (September 26, Old Style) on John the Theologian's feast day, I am forty-eight years old. I congratulate myself—knock on wood—for getting well, and maybe for forty-eight years of a soul's uninterrupted existence.

My difficulty (in writing poems—and perhaps other people's difficulty in understanding them) is in the impossibility of my goal, for example, to use words to express a moan: *nnh, nnh, nnh.* To express a sound using words, using meanings. So that the only thing left in the ears would be *nnh, nnh, nnh.*

WRITING BOOKS AND NOTEBOOKS, SEPTEMBER 1940

AFTERWORD

"There cannot be too much of lyric because lyric itself is too much."

—TSVETAEVA

1.

As a child, Marina Tsvetaeva had "a frenzied wish to become lost" in the city of Moscow. As a girl, she dreamed of being adopted by the devil in Moscow streets, of being the devil's little orphan. But Russian poetry began in St. Petersburg—the new capital was founded in the early eighteenth century. Moscow was the old capital, devoid of literature. No literature existed in Russia before St. Petersburg's cosmopolitan streets.

But St. Petersburg was also, for two hundred years, the least free city in Russia. It was dominated by the secret police, watched by the Tsar, and full of soldiers and civil servants—the city of loneliness Dostoevsky and Gogol shared with us.

Moscow was for a long time the seat of the old Russia that considered

St. Petersburg blasphemous. Moscow was the center of Russia without professors, without foreigners; it was the Russia where the Tsar was still thought to be divine. Peter the Great's unloved first wife, speaking from Moscow, put a curse on St. Petersburg, saying that it would "stand empty."

In the middle of this Moscow, Marina Tsvetaeva wanted a desk.

2.

For her, a desk was the first and only musical instrument.[1] Tsvetaeva said her first language was not Russian speech; it was music. Her first word, spoken at the age of one, was "gamma" or "scale."[2] But music was difficult. "You press on a key on a piano," she said remembering her childhood. "A key is right there, here, black or white, but a note? . . . But one day I saw instead of notes sitting on the staff, there were—sparrows! Then I realized that musical notes live on branches, each one on its own, and from there they jump onto the keys, each one onto its own. And then—it sounds. When I stop playing music the notes return on the branches—as birds go to sleep."[3]

Marina Tsvetaeva's mother was a talented musician. But when Marina was still very young, her mother was already ill. The illness made them travel from one city to another, from one country to the next. On the road, Marina Tsvetaeva learned German, Italian, then French. She wrote poems in French as well as German; her grandfather recited German poetry by heart. Her mother's illness was a carriage which took her, for years, across Europe.

But her mother wanted to die at home, in Russia. So in 1906, mother and daughter Tsvetaeva started for Moscow. Her mother died on the road, not reaching the city. Tsvetaeva was 14.

3.

So how do we explain that the poet whom Pasternak called "the most Russian of all Russian poets" spent much of her developmental years in Germany, France, and Italy? How come she called—insisted on calling— German her "native language"? Perhaps this is because poets are not born in a country. Poets are born in childhood. Perhaps because Marina Tsvetaeva was able to speak in more than one language, she was able to keep "secrets," "empty pockets," or as Emily Dickinson would put it, "slants," in the Russian language. But how do we explain this effect on the Russian readers, in an altogether new language, English? Perhaps a story could help:

. . . speaking of their journey back to Russia, Tsvetaeva remembered how her mother, dying, "stood up and, refusing support, took those few steps by herself, towards the piano for her last practice, whispering, 'Well, let's see what I am still able to do?' She was smiling and, it was clear, talking to herself. She sat down. Everyone stood. And there, from her hands already out of practice—but I don't want to name the music yet, that is still the secret I have with her."[4]

4.

How did she write?

Sweeping away all affairs, from early morning, with a clear head, on an empty stomach. With a cup of boiling black coffee on the writing desk, to which each day of her life she walked like a worker to a machine.

Everything on the desk was swept away—a place for a notebook and two elbows.

Deafened and blind to all around her. Never wrote on separate pages, only a notebook; all kinds of notebooks, schoolbooks, accountants' books.

A puff on a cigarette. A gulp of coffee. Mumbling, trying the words in her mouth.

Answered letters right away, writing her response upon arrival. Saw her letters as a craft almost as necessary to her as her poems.

Closing the notebook she opened the door to her room.[5]

5.

Not long after Tsvetaeva's mother died, her father opened a museum of fine arts in the middle of peasant Russia—Russia of factory workers, of hunger strikes, of bloody uprisings, of the First World War. In the middle of this country, between two revolutions, Tsvetaeva and her younger sister grew up inside a museum.

It was Russia's first ever Museum of Fine Arts. "Why build a museum?" newspapers of that time exclaimed. "We need hospitals, schools, scientific labs." And other newspapers countered, "Let them build! Once the Revolution comes, we'll throw out the statues and put school desks, hospital beds there. The walls will be useful!"

Tsvetaeva recited these curses by heart, years later. After decades, she remembered it, this building. The museum. She called it Brother.

She remembered the opening of the museum: it was a moment of civil unrest, but she was watching the charming ladies, the Tsar himself cutting the ribbons. Long after the Revolution, she compared the museum's opening to Kitezh, the mystical Russian city whose inhabitants, according to the legend, decided that the city must fall through the earth and hide underground to escape the invasion.

6.

A few years after her mother's death, Marina Tsvetaeva, still a young schoolgirl, published her first book. Critics praised the book's uncommon "intimacy of tone" and its structure, called it a lyric diary, a daybook, a sequence;[6] they praised the "bravery" of this "intimacy."[7]

There was also criticism. Brusov, the venerable older poet, encouraged her poems' "sense of intimacy" but noted that this lyric intimacy was, sometimes—often—too much.

But there cannot be "too much" of lyric because lyric itself is "too much." Tsvetaeva: "A lyric poem is a created and instantly destroyed world. How many poems are in the book—that many explosions, fires, eruptions: EMPTY spaces. The lyric poem—is a catastrophe. It barely began—and already ended."[8]

7.

So here is a poet who claims that her first language was music and her "native language was German," and this poet is called, by Pasternak, "more Russian than all of us." What, then, is her work like in Russian? Khodosevich:

Tsvetaeva understood the audial and linguistic work that play such an enormous role in folk song. Folk song is in large part a litany, joyful or grieving. There is an element of lamentation, an element of tongue-twister and pun, there are echoes of spell, incantation, even exorcism in a folk song—there is a pure play of sounds—it is always partly hysterical, nearly a fall into crying or laughter, and partly zaum.[*]

Admiring her, the poet Balmont once said, "You demand from poetry what only music can give."

Was she a 'difficult' poet? Perhaps. But first we must clarify what 'difficult' meant for that country and that time. To clarify this, one turns to Pushkin, the father of the Russian poetic tradition:

One of our poets used to say proudly, "Though some of my verses may be obscure they are never prosaic." There are two kinds of obscurity; one arises from a lack of feelings and thoughts, which have been replaced by words; the other from an abundance of feelings and thoughts, and the inadequacy of words to express them.[9]

8.

So how does one attempt to translate the work that even poets of Russia find too demanding? Translators usually cite Tsvetaeva's famous temperament. "Next time I will be born not on a planet, but on a comet!" she wrote. With bravery, they announce their ambition to imitate her music in English—to stay "faithful" to the music.

---

* *zaum* refers to the pure play of language, "beyonsense"

Merely acknowledging an attempt to imitate Tsvetaeva's sounds produces just that: an attempt at imitation that cannot rise to the level of the original. This may occur because of the translator's lack of skill or because the "receiving" language, English, is an entirely different medium at a very different point in its development, a point at which the particular sound effects mean entirely different things.

We *do not* claim to do better. In fact, Jean Valentine and I do not claim to have translated her. To translate is to inhabit. The meaning of the word *ekstasis* is to stand outside of one's body. This we do not claim. (We wish we could, one day.) Jean Valentine and I claim we are two poets who fell in love with a third and spent two years reading her together. If translation—as most translators are eager to claim—is "a closest possible reading," then this is not translation; it is a notation, a midrash. These pages are fragments, notes in the margin. "Erase everything you have written," Mandelstam says, "but keep the notes in the margin."

So, what is this enterprise? Our two temperaments differ vastly from Tsvetaeva's, but we are drawn by her magnetism and so we continue reading her together. Just that: reading lines, fragments, moments; two years of two poets reading a third is an homage.

What would Tsvetaeva herself think of the many English translations of her work? She translated Rilke, famously. She translated Shakespeare, too, and Rostan, and Lorca—into Russian. She also translated Mayakovsky, Pushkin, and Lermontov into French. She translated herself into French as well, devoting a great deal of time and care to it. Was she faithful? Not at all. She also translated from languages she did not know: Georgian, Polish, Yiddish. Most of her translations are far from literal. "I tried to translate," she wrote, "but then decided—why should I get in my own way? Moreover, there is a lot the French would not understand which is clear to us. The result was I *rewrote* it."

Scholars call her best work of translation—her take on Baudelaire's "Voyage"—a work translated "not from French into Russian" but from "Baudelaire into Tsvetaeva."

9.

In 1940, when asked for her favorite authors, Tsvetaeva named these three: Selma Ottilia Lovisa Lagerlöf (Swedish children's author of *The Wonderful Adventures of Nils*), Sigrid Undset (Norwegian author of novels about Scandinavia in the Middle Ages, who died in a Nazi camp), and Mary Webb (English novelist).

This list begs a question: but what about her numerous, famously longish poem-cycles for other poets? She barely knew most of them in person. Relationships took place at a distance:

Rilke whom she never met,
Blok, with whom she never spoke,
Akhmatova whom she barely knew,
Mayakovsky whom she knew in passing (she called him "dear enemy"),
and Pasternak whom she knew mostly through correspondence.

(One begins to think of Fernando Pessoa and his various masks, or Borges and his imaginary library: their bent of imagination, that is, combined with Dickinson's intensity of form.)

At the turn of the century Russian literature was the land of many literary movements—Akhmatova, Mandelstam and Gumiliov were the Akhmeist poets; Blok was the Symbolist poet; Khlebnikhov, Kruchenukh, Mayakovsky, Aseev—even Pasternak began in the same innovative group. Marina Tsvetaeva stood outside of all groups or manifestoes.

Tsvetaeva found the fellowship not of poets, but of their work: "Akhmatova," "Mayakovsky," "Essenin," "Pushkin," "Pasternak," "Blok"—it was not the real people who lived sometimes only a few streets away from her, but their work that led Tsvetaeva to imagine them and dedicate her own best poems to them.

For a lyric poet, education happens not in a group, not in an MFA program or a classroom, but in one place: the library. Teachers and groups give us rules. Books and poems give us opportunities, possibilities for the expansion of craft.

Tsvetaeva created a Kitezh of poets. She absorbed and extended their poetics. Her work of dedication, of homage to other poets, is really an example of *ekstasis*. It extends to her very grammar, with its unbridled inversions. Her hurried, gulping syntax erases the unnecessary, the trifles and chitchat are gone. Her dashes jump from breath to breath, syntax falls apart and is hammered into rhymes.

This wasn't to everyone's taste. When Pasternak, worried about her poverty, wrote to Gorky, praising Tsvetaeva's linguistic talent, begging for help, Gorky disagreed, stating, "She has a poor command of speech, speech commands her."[10] Her lyricism—for the leader of Social Realists—was too much.

10.

Tsvetaeva always carried a notebook in her bag and thought it necessary to write everything down. She repeated to all of us: do this. She wrote down dreams, conversations, arguments, thoughts about work. She had large notebooks, small notebooks in which she rewrote, and final notebooks.[11]

For years, she carried in her bag a letter she wrote, but never mailed, to Anna Akhmatova. At this point, one may add that when Russian critics speak about Akhmatova and Tsvetaeva they speak of them as opposites, polarities, but we shall remember what they shared.

Tsvetaeva writes:
Little town in bird-cherry trees, in wattles, in soldiers' overcoats.
1916. People walk to war.[12]

Akhmatova writes:
Downcast eyes, dry
and wringing her hands, Russia
before me walked to the east.[13]

11.

What Akhmatova and Tsvetaeva shared was the equation of "poet vs. state," which, in Russia, goes way back:

Vasily Trediakovsky, early Russian poet and author of the first text
on poetics, was a court poet; "when an official demanded an ode on

the occasion of some holiday—but the ode was not ready in time; the
fiery official punished the negligent poet with the rod."[14]

In a sense, for the poet of that time, the Revolution was the return of
the darkness, and the freedom, of Muscovy.

During 1917, Tsvetaeva lived in Moscow, a city where with "such
grave attentiveness they ride a sleigh with a little food package and
such cheerful carelessness they sleigh with a coffin."

That year, she had an occasion to read together with Lunacharsky,
the People's Commissar of Education. What did she do with the Party
Boss seated in the first row? She recited the words of a character
awaiting execution at the hands of revolutionaries, and later she
reflected on the experience of that recital: "Never did I breathe with
such a sense of responsibility. A nobleman's soliloquy right into the
commissar's face—this is what I call life!"[15]

In those years, she shared her meager food supply with an older ailing
poet, Balmont; she made appointments to see Lunacharsky to beg for help
for starving writers in Crimea. In those years, she asked for the ability to
"live as I write: spare—the way / God asks me—and friends do not."

And what was it like to give a poetry reading during the Russian
Revolution? What may we imagine when we think of her voice during
those years? During the Revolution, Tsvetaeva had a habit of bringing
her younger sister to the public readings and reciting her poems in
unison with her.

Their voices sounded identical.

12

One great poet of her generation Tsvetaeva did meet; in 1916, she met young Osip Mandelstam. They had a brief affair during the Civil War. Mandelstam visited her so often—by train from St. Petersburg—that one friend joked, "I wonder if he is working for the railways." Years later, Nadezhda Mandelstam, the poet's widow, recalled:

The friendship with Tsvetaeva, in my opinion, played an enormous role for Mandelstam's work. It was a bridge on which he walked from one period of his work to another. With poems to Tsvetaeva begins his second book of poems, Tristia. *Mandelstam's first book,* Stone, *was the restrained, elegant work of a Petersburg poet. Tsvetaeva's friendship gave him her Moscow, lifting the spell of Petersburg's elegance. It was a magical gift, because with Petersburg alone, without Moscow, there is no freedom of full breath, no true feeling of Russia, no conscience. I am sure that my own relationship with Mandelstam would not have been the same if on his path he had not met, so bright and wild, Marina. She opened in him the love of life, the ability for spontaneous and unbridled love of life, which struck me from the first minute I saw him.*

According to Mme. Mandelstam, "Tsvetaeva had a generosity of soul and a selflessness which had no equal. It was directed by her willfulness and impetuosity, which too, had no equal."[16]

13.

A fact: the Revolution brought Tsvetaeva poverty and the five-year-long absence of her husband, who joined the White Army and fought the Revolutionaries in Crimea and elsewhere.

A fact: after the Revolution, Tsvetaeva almost starved. She left both of her daughters in an orphanage where it was said they would be better fed, and one of them, the younger, Irina, died of starvation.

When my child died in Russia from hunger and I learnt of this— simply on the street from a strange person—("Little Irina your daughter?—Yes—She died. Yesterday died. Tomorrow we will bury her.")—and I kept silent three months—not a word of death—to anyone—so she [the child] did not die finally, and still (in me)— lived. This is why your Rilke did not mention my name. To name [call/speak]—is to take apart: to separate self from thing. I don't name anyone—ever.[17]

This too, is a lesson found in her poetics: Marina Tsvetaeva, the poet so obsessed with the Russian language, *the* Russian poet of her generation, the poet who wrote elegies for everyone else—including the living—at her own elegiac moment, chose *not* to speak.

14.

"I can eat—with dirty hands, sleep—with dirty hands, write with dirty hands I cannot. (In Soviet Russia, when there was no water, I licked my hands.)"[18]

What did she do with those circumstances? She sat at her desk and wrote by hand over a thousand texts.

15.

On August 2, 1921 Nikolai Gumiliov, who was Akhmatova's husband and a prominent poet, was arrested and subsequently shot. On August 7, Alexander Blok, forty-one years old, died in a state of despair bordering on insanity. At the end of August, rumors circulated that Akhmatova had killed herself. (Mayakovsky organized a chain of friends to discover the truth and dispel rumors. In gratitude, Tsvetaeva dedicated a poem to him, calling him "heavy-footed archangel.") In early 1922, the great Futurist poet Velemir Khlebnikhov died.

In 1922, the Communists ordered two hundred philosophers, scientists, and writers to board a ship. Subsequently called The Philosophers' Ship, it included every single prominent non-Marxist philosopher in Russia. All were sent into exile.

Marina Tsvetaeva left Russia in the spring of that year; she stepped off the train in Berlin on May 15, 1922.

16

Can a poem by Tsvetaeva be translated?

No.

Do we, as English-speaking poets, benefit from the infusion of her poetic world-view—her metaphysics, so to speak—into our work?

Yes.

Consider her metaphysics.

First, an aside: in her toughest years in emigration, when many turned away, one of the few persons who kept in touch with Tsvetaeva was Lev Shestov (Yehuda Leyb Shwarzmann), who like Tsvetaeva, had benefited hugely from the advantages of Russia's "cultural time lag": no centuries of philosophy in the past. Because of this "cultural time lag," Shestov "didn't care whether what he was saying about Plato or Spinoza was against the rules of the game."

What does the creature that calls itself "I" want for itself? It wants to be. Quite a demand!

The "I" has to recognize that it is confronted with a world that follows its own laws, a world whose name is Necessity. This, according to Shestov, is the foundation of philosophy... "I" must accept the inevitable order of the world. In simple language, "grin and bear it"; in a more sophisticated language, "The fates lead the willing man; they drag the unwilling."

This is the idea of stoicism that is at the core of much of western culture. Shestov refuses it:

[He] refuses to play this game. For why should the "I" accept "wisdom," which obviously violates its most intense desire? Isn't there something horrible in Spinoza's advice to philosophers: "Not to laugh, not to weep, not to hate, but to understand."

On the contrary, says Shestov, a man should shout, scream, laugh, jeer, protest.[19]

Though not aimed at her, these words also describe Tsvetaeva's metaphysics. Tsvetaeva, too, "loved only those who, like Pascal, 'seek while moaning.'"[20]

17.

Having arrived abroad, Tsvetaeva wrote, "My motherland is any place with a writing desk, a window, and a tree by that window." She wrote of exile: "For lyric poets and fairy-tale authors, it is better that they see their motherland from afar—from a great distance."

Compare this to Gogol: " . . . my nature is the ability to imagine a world graphically only when I have moved far away from it. That is why I can write about Russia only in Rome. Only there does it stand before me in all its hugeness."[21]

Again, Tsvetaeva: "Russia (the sound of the word) no longer exists, there exist four letters: USSR—I cannot and will not go where there are no vowels, into those whistling consonants. And, they won't let me there, the letters won't open."

So Tsvetaeva spent seventeen years in France. France did not allow foreigners to have regular jobs and papers were hard to obtain. But

Paris had a large concentration of journals, publishing houses, and émigré intellectuals. Tsvetaeva wrote, "I get numerous invitations, but I cannot show myself because there is no silk dress, no stockings, no patent leather shoes, which is the local uniform. So I stay at home, accused from all sides of being too proud."[22]

After Hitler assumed power in Germany, the USSR began to look brighter to many émigrés. After much family drama (which we need not explore here), Tsvetaeva, without any particular nostalgic feeling, returned to Moscow on June 18, 1939.

18.

Barely a few weeks after her return to the USSR, Tsvetaeva's relatives were arrested. A few weeks passed. More arrests. After the arrests, she began to wander all over Moscow, from one friend's flat to the next. Tsvetaeva stood in lines outside of prison walls. As long as parcels were accepted, the loved one was presumed alive.

What *is* the Tsvetaeva myth? A poet whose life (and language, though you can't see it in translation) was radical, strange, and unlike anyone else's, and yet whose life is so representative of her time.

A woman who escapes and runs and yells and pauses and stands in silence—silence, which is the soul's noise: "But we stand up—as long as there's spit in our mouths!"

Even her suicide becomes a metaphor for the civic suicide of a century that sent to death millions of its inhabitants.

August 31, 1941. The poet killed herself on the last day of summer.

What then, is the lyric poet's attitude toward her or his time?

Tsvetaeva wrote, "You can't buy me. That is the whole point. To buy is to buy oneself off. You can't buy yourself off from me. You can buy me only with the whole sky in yourself. The whole sky in which, perhaps, there is no place for me."

This is not a question of biography, personality, or personal life. It is a craft question, a question of *tone*.

But what goals can one have as one deals with the difficulty of translating this tone? What, exactly, is the difficulty? Here is a page from one of Tsvetaeva's final notebooks, which may provide a hint:

Today (September 26, Old Style) on John the Theologian's feast day, I am forty-eight years old. I congratulate myself—knock on wood—for getting well, and maybe for forty-eight years of a soul's uninterrupted existence.

My difficulty (in writing poems—and perhaps other people's difficulty in understanding them) is in the impossibility of my goal, for example, to use words to express a moan: nnh, nnh, nnh. To express a sound using words, using meanings. So that the only thing left in the ears would be nnh, nnh, nnh.

—ILYA KAMINSKY

1 Ariadna Efron, "Solonim," *Vospominania o Marine Tsvetaevoi*, ed. Turchinksky Mukhin (Moscow: Soviet Writer Publishers, 1992).
2 Marina Tsvetaeva, "Mother and Music," *Sobranie Sochinenii* (Moscow: Terra Publishers, 1997).
3 Ibid.
4 Ibid.
5 Ariadna Efron, *Vospominania o Marine Tsvetaevoi*, ed. Turchinksky Mukhin (Moscow: Soviet Writer Publishers, 1992).
6 Maximilian Voloshin, "Poetry by Women," *Morning of Russia*, December 11, 1910.
7 Nikolai Gumiliov, "Essays and Notes on Russian Poetry," *Appolo #5*, 1911.
8 Marina Tsvetaeva, *Sobranie Sochinenii* (Moscow: Terra Publishers, 1997).
9 Aleksander Pushkin, *The Critical Prose of Alexander Pushkin*, ed. Carl Proffer (Bloomington: Indiana University Press, 1969).
10 Simon Karlinsky, *Marina Tsvetaeva: The Woman, Her World, and Her Poetry* (Cambridge: Cambridge University Press, 1986).
11 Ariadna Efron, *Vospominania o Marine Tsvetaevoi*, ed. Turchinksky Mukhin (Moscow: Soviet Writer Publishers, 1992).
12 Marina Tsvetaeva, "History of One Dedication," *Sobranie Sochinenii* (Moscow: Terra Publishers, 1997).
13 Anna Akhmatova, "Poem Without a Hero," *Maloe Sobranie Sochinenii* (Moscow: Azbuka Publishers, 2012).
14 Aleksander Pushkin, *Pushkin on Literature*, ed. Tatiana Wolf (London: Athlone Press, 2000).
15 Marina Tsvetaeva, "My jobs," *Sobranie Sochinenii* (Moscow: Terra Publishers, 1997).
16 Nadezhda Mandelstam, *Hope Abandoned* (New York: Scribner, 1981).
17 Rainer Maria Rilke, "Rainer Maria Rilke und Marina Zwetajewa: Ein Gesprach in Briefen," *Herausgegeben von Konstantin Asadowski* (Frankfurt/Main und Laipzig: Insel Verlag, 1992).
18 Marina Tsvetaeva, "History of One Dedication," *Sobranie Sochinenii* (Moscow: Terra Publishers, 1997).
19 Czeslaw Milosz, "Shestov, or the Purity of Despair," *To Begin Where I Am: Selected Essays* (New York: FSG, 2001).
20 Ibid.
21 Nikolai Gogol, *Letters of Nikolai Gogol*, ed. Carl Proffer (Ann Arbor: University of Michigan Press, 1967).
22 Simon Karlinsky, *Marina Tsvetaeva: The Woman, Her World, and Her Poetry* (Cambridge: Cambridge University Press, 1986).

ABOUT THE INTRODUCTION

Stephanie Sandler is an Ernest E. Monrad Professor in the Slavic Department at Harvard University. Alongside strong interests in film, cultural theory, and translation, she writes about Russian poetry, with a focus on contemporary writers. Commemorating Pushkin: Russia's Myth of a National Poet appeared from Stanford Press in 2004; her translation, with Genya Turovskaya, of The Russian Version by contemporary Moscow poet Elena Fanailova appeared in 2010. Recent translations have appeared in *The Boston Review, Poetry, Fence, Guernica*, and *World Literature Today*.

RECENT TITLES FROM ALICE JAMES BOOKS

Tantivy, Donald Revell
Murder Ballad, Jane Springer
Sudden Dog, Matthew Pennock
Western Practice, Stephen Motika
me and Nina, Monica A. Hand
Hagar Before the Occupation | Hagar After the Occupation, Amal al-Jubouri
Pier, Janine Oshiro
Heart First into the Forest, Stacy Gnall
This Strange Land, Shara McCallum
lie down too, Lesle Lewis
Panic, Laura McCullough
Milk Dress, Nicole Cooley
Parable of Hide and Seek, Chad Sweeney
Shahid Reads His Own Palm, Reginald Dwayne Betts
How to Catch a Falling Knife, Daniel Johnson
Phantom Noise, Brian Turner
Father Dirt, Mihaela Moscaliuc
Pageant, Joanna Fuhrman
The Bitter Withy, Donald Revell
Winter Tenor, Kevin Goodan
Slamming Open the Door, Kathleen Sheeder Bonanno
Rough Cradle, Betsy Sholl
Shelter, Carey Salerno
The Next Country, Idra Novey
Begin Anywhere, Frank Giampietro
The Usable Field, Jane Mead

Alice James Books has been publishing poetry since 1973 and remains one of the few presses in the country that is run collectively. The cooperative selects manuscripts for publication primarily through regional and national annual competitions. Authors who win a Kinereth Gensler Award become active members of the cooperative board and participate in the editorial decisions of the press. The press, which historically has placed an emphasis on publishing women poets, was named for Alice James, sister of William and Henry, whose fine journal and gift for writing went unrecognized during her lifetime.

Designed by Mary Austin Speaker